Evangel
the
Fringe

John Clarke

Vicar of St Mary's, Greenham

GROVE BOOKS LIMITED

BRAMCOTE NOTTINGHAM NG9 3DS

Contents

The Cover Illustration is by Peter Ashton

First Impression May 1995
ISSN 0953-4946
ISBN 1 85174 290 5

1
Introduction

The fringe is the fishing pool of evangelism. It is widely recognised that this pool, at least as far as occasional church-goers are concerned, has shrunk rapidly in Britain in recent years. Both its size and shape have changed. How should we adjust our fishing methods as a result?

This booklet has been based on a two year part-time research project looking at how a church's evangelism strategy needs to vary to take account of local conditions and culture, and particularly the nature of the pattern of relationships existing between the church and its local community. Much of the research was of an informal nature, being based on interviews with ministers and others. It also consisted of two surveys. The first, which was more detailed, was sent to members of the British Church Growth Association. This group, from a mainly evangelical constituency, produced 48 replies providing an analysis of how more than 1000 people had become Christians in the last five years. The second, less detailed, survey was sent to ministers of broader church tradition, and 66 replies were received. The full results are set out in much more detail in my book *Evangelism that Really Works*.[1]

One vital conclusion of the research was that the nature of a church's fringe should be a key determinant of evangelistic strategy. It is my conviction that failure to understand this is having an adverse effect on many churches' evangelism. In this booklet, we shall look first of all at the nature of the fringe; this will enable us to identify four alternative 'models' or patterns of evangelism which operate in different churches. We shall then consider a limited sample of approaches to evangelism that have worked in different cultures. Finally, we shall consider how a church can start to draw up a strategy, taking account of the nature of its fringe.

1 J Clarke, *Evangelism that Really Works* (London: SPCK, June 1995).

2
Journey Into Faith

There has been renewed emphasis in recent years on the fact that coming to faith is a process. We can call it a 'journey.' People are at different stages on that journey, and so are at different distances from Christian commitment. The journey may start with experiencing the love of Christians, or possibly at a crisis event such as a bereavement or the birth of a child. Later stages in the journey will almost certainly include attending church and receiving some Christian teaching. Sometimes, near the end of the journey, there is a 'Damascus Road' experience when much that has been previously learned or experienced suddenly makes sense, and they 'commit their life to Christ.'

Many of those in the fringe are people on a journey. Hopefully it is a journey towards faith. Some, sadly, may have decided they have gone as far as they wish to. Others may be less committed now than in the past. Nevertheless, in normal circumstances, a reasonable percentage of the fringe will be travelling towards, and have some openness to, Christian faith.

The insight that the fringe consists at least partly of people on a journey will be important for our evangelism. It will be more about process, about helping people forward on their journey, than about producing instant conversions—though this will have its place, too. The Church Growth school has produced some useful categories for describing the different emphases needed in evangelism at differing stages of the journey.

Presence evangelism refers to Christian witness, primarily by deed in a community. In a local church, it might involve starting an advice centre or a parent and toddler group. It could also include the love and care shown by individual Christians, possibly in the context of a church activity. *Proclamation* evangelism involves teaching or explaining the gospel message. This could include anything from a sermon to a Bible study course to a conversation over dinner. *Persuasion* evangelism refers to the process of discussion and questioning that takes place, usually at the end of a faith journey, when someone is thinking about becoming a Christian. It includes both church run enquirers' groups, and also late night cups of coffee!

Usually, the '3 P's of evangelism apply at particular stages in the faith journey. Presence evangelism comes first. Most people have no serious interest in the gospel message until they experience the love of Jesus in a Christian or through a church community. Next comes proclamation. It is often at this stage that 'something clicks' and the person starts enquiring in earnest. Persuasion (not the best word, I'll admit) is the final stage. Clearly, many of the fringe are at the 'presence' or first stage in their faith journey.

3
Types of Fringe

What exactly is the fringe? It is all those who feel positive about the Church. It includes those who attend occasionally, such as at major festivals; those contacted through baptisms, weddings and funerals; those who take the parish magazine; those who belong to church organisations or whose children attend the youth groups; and also those who are simply friends or relatives of church members.

Bishop Gavin Reid has suggested two categories of fringe:

- The *Institutional* fringe, who relate in some way to the Church as an institution;
- The *Personal* fringe, who are the personal friends and relatives of Church members.

We shall see that it is important to make this distinction when we come to consider appropriate ways of evangelizing the fringe.

We have already seen that many of the fringe have at least some warmth towards Christian faith. Nevertheless, their openness towards going further may vary dramatically. Some may be genuinely open to real Christian commitment, and simply need the gospel to be presented in a way which they understand. Others, though, will have travelled as far as they want to. They do not want to get drawn in too far, or to become 'fanatical'—they are 'steadfast and immovable,' just a few yards outside the Kingdom of God!

It may, therefore, be helpful to make a further distinction between:

- the *Open* fringe, who should be the priority in our evangelism; and
- the *Closed* fringe, whom it may be wise to leave fallow for another year.

4
Models of Church

When I started my research I expected to find that the prime influence on evangelism strategy would be local culture. The rural church would be very different from an inner city one, and so forth. I expected to produce lists of approaches which would work best in different cultural settings. In fact, I discovered that the diversity of cultures was greater than I had realized. Two council estates next door to each other, or two villages only a few miles apart, could be radically different from each other. In the end, my unexpected conclusion was that, rather than culture *per se*, a key factor was *the pattern of relationships existing between the church and the local community*. I have attempted to express this in terms of four models.

The Osmosis Church

Under this model, there is a reluctance to count some 'out' and others 'in.' The emphasis is on process rather than crisis. Many in the neighbourhood may view the church as 'theirs,' and the priest or minister sees his or her job as drawing them towards the centre. The church is seen as a church for the area, rather than exclusively for its own congregation. The classic case must surely be the Anglican village church, but many churches from other denominations and situated in different cultures see themselves as operating under this model.

Such churches need to keep open boundaries. Attitudes need to be open too! Catholics and liberals are often better at this than evangelicals. Some evangelical congregations are so keen to get people converted, that they can appear confrontational and threatening. Such churches soon lose their fringe.

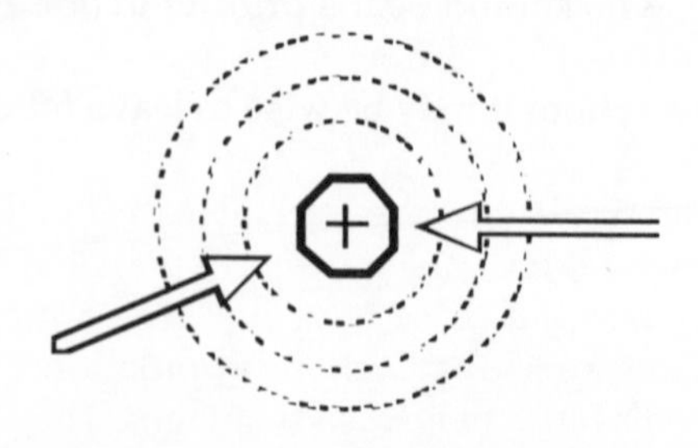

Diagram 1: The Osmosis Model

The Osmosis church has many strengths. It is the best model for providing 'salt and light' in a modest sized local community. By taking the local area seriously, and not simply trying to save individuals, it pays proper attention to Jesus' teaching on the Kingdom of God.

I believe there are two facets of modern British society which are making the Osmosis church less effective in many areas than it has been in the past. First, it requires a reasonably developed sense of community, preferably with the church having a central role. This applied in every case for the churches in my research which were evangelizing effectively using the Osmosis model. Second, there must be at least some nominal faith amongst the people it is trying to serve. Both these features are in decline in Britain today.

The Web Church

The Web church grows along natural relationship networks, and for this reason often draws in like-minded people. Web churches thrive best in car culture, where they can draw on a massive population. Well known examples include city centre churches, often with many students and young professionals, and also ethnic churches. I had not realized that virtually all the black-led churches in this country are in fact Webs drawing from a distance. It is easy to see why. Kinship and friendship links are strong within any minority group, and it is just these links which make for a strong Web church.

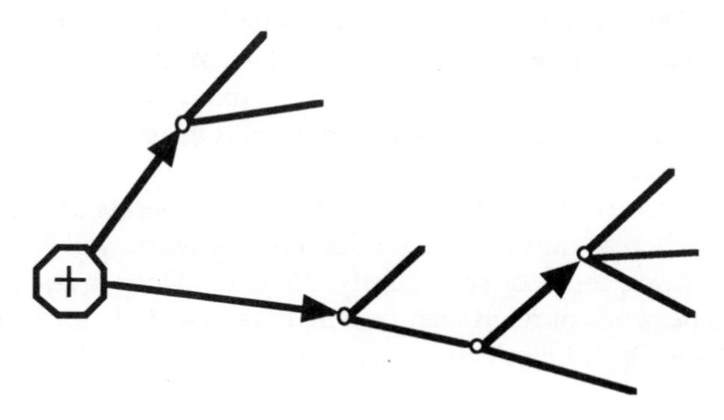

Diagram 2: The Web Model

Web churches can be extremely powerful in evangelism. Most of the largest British churches are Webs. The only exceptions I know of are some very large Catholic churches, but these have not grown mainly by evangelism, but by attracting a large existing Catholic population.

Nevertheless, Webs have some disadvantages. They have been criticized in the past, with some validity, as being proselytizers which do little to serve society. Those committed to a Kingdom theology, and the notion of serving a parish, have found them hard to accept. Increasingly, though, the best Web churches are taking social action seriously, though it is sometimes city-wide rather than geared to the immediate locality.

In some contexts the successful Web church can actually be off-putting to its local community. Village people can find it puzzling seeing the cars drawing up from far afield. They no longer feel it is 'their church.' They are suspicious. 'Lots of people come in cars from a long way away and give 'im lots of money. There's summat strange about that church.' A woman in her twenties was speaking about the 'other church' in the village.

There is another side to this coin, though. Osmosis churches, while supposedly catering for all in a local community, can, in reality, exclude some groups. They are not necessarily attractive, for example, to single adults in their twenties. Yet Web churches can attract this group in large numbers.

The Osmosis and Web models, which we have just considered, were the first two models which emerged from my research. As the work progressed, however, it became clear that many churches did not really fit either model. Several other models emerged, the two most important being variations on the Osmosis and Web.

The Open Door Model

Like the Osmosis model, the Open Door draws on the Institutional fringe. Whereas in an Osmosis church people find their way in through a variety of routes, in an Open Door church there are usually one or two main ways in. There are a wide variety of *possible* open doors. What the research showed was that, in practice, only one or two were likely to be open for a given church. These could be, for example, preparation for infant baptism or a particularly successful community group.

The importance of the Open Door is that it can operate in a wider variety of contexts. Whereas the Osmosis model can only work well where there is a reasonably strong sense of community, the Open Door is less restricted. A strong local network of relationships will, of course, help any form of evangelism, but the Open Door can survive without it—providing it can find an open door.

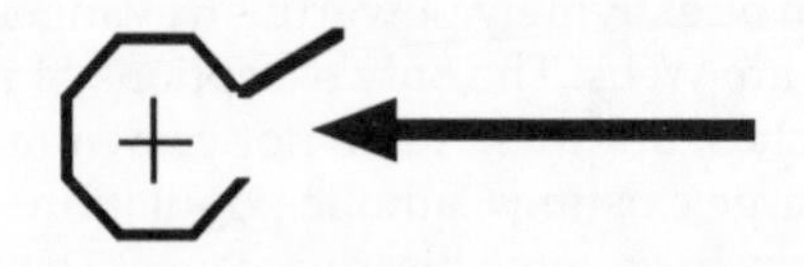

Diagram 3: The Open Door Church

The Stepping Stones Church

The Stepping Stones church is really a variation of the Web, enabling it to operate in a smaller and less receptive population. Like the Web, it draws on a Personal fringe, but rather than inviting contacts mainly to church services, an array of other events is organized. These may range from purely social occasions to evangelistic meals with a speaker, and take account of the fact that many, including the proverbial non-Christian husband, may have an attitude block as far as church services are concerned. Such folk will be more willing to come to events and, provided they meet Christians they can relate to and respect, they may well come to faith in gentle steps, whereas it would be too much to expect them to attend church in one jump.

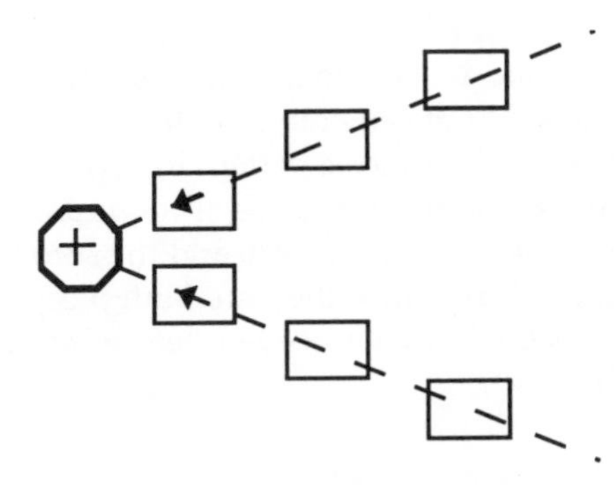

Diagram 4: The Stepping Stones Model

Two further points need to be made. First, the models are descriptions of particular patterns of evangelism dynamics. Many churches, naturally, will not fit any one pure pattern. Many will be hybrids. I can think, for example, of one 'new' church which mainly fits the Stepping Stones pattern, and arranges many dinners and other social events to exploit its Personal fringe. It also organizes one or two community groups in order to create an Institutional fringe, and hopefully some open doors. In some cases, though, this can create an awkward tension in the church's life.

I have recently become vicar of St Mary's, Greenham, near Newbury. The church is strongly charismatic with a largely eclectic congregation. The existing evangelism dynamic has been largely on the basis of a Web model, with members of the congregation inviting friends to services of a strongly spiritual nature. My difficulty is that, if we are to build up an Institutional fringe and start to draw in people from our own parish, much more low key services will almost certainly be needed. It is very difficult to reconcile the two underlying dynamics. We are praying hard!

The point I am making is that, though a degree of compromise between the models may be possible, hard choices will sometimes need to be made. That is why I believe it is essential for churches to understand their current dynamic, and to think through clearly whether it is the right one.

The second point is that some churches do not fit any model. Each of the models assumes that evangelism is going on according to some consistent pattern. That, of course, is not always the case. I call such churches 'Sleeping Giants' but you could argue that they are really examples of any of the four models held back by some constraint. This need not imply any lack of spiritual vigour in the church. Take, for example, an inner city free church with a largely elderly eclectic congregation—probably people who have lived in the area and belonged to the church in their younger days before prospering and moving out. Such a church will find it desperately difficult to build up an Institutional fringe, and its Personal fringe will not be effective in evangelism either. Or take an Anglican church with a largely pastoral ministry attempting to operate on the Osmosis pattern in a sprawling suburb split by major roads where there is almost no sense of community. The first of these, being eclectic, might look more like a Web and the second more like an Osmosis model church, but in reality they are both Sleeping Giants. In each case some tough decisions may be needed before the church can become effective in evangelism.

5
Evangelizing the Institutional Fringe

In this chapter, and the next, we look at a few practical examples—building blocks for producing a strategy. They can be no more than 'tasters.' Those included will be dealt with briefly. Inevitably I have had to include some areas and ignore others. A fuller treatment is given in *Evangelism that Really Works.*

We have already seen that many Osmosis churches need to develop some 'open doors.'[2] In theory, one would like an open door in virtually every area in the Church's life, but the sheer time and resources available may preclude this. It may be necessary to identify the one or two most likely open doors and concentrate on them at least for the time being.

We now consider some examples of evangelizing the Institutional fringe. Mostly they constitute 'open doors.'

The General Service Fringe

Under the Osmosis model, do people just drift into faith, or does the church have to *do* something? Unquestionably, some will simply drift into faith. In my research, of just over 1000 people who had become Christians, general involvement in church and services was a key factor in coming to faith for 138, and often the only one listed.

Nevertheless, it is widely recognized today that if we simply let people drift, some will be lost and others will only limp along in the faith. The role of some kind of enquirers' or nurture group is crucial. The important thing for the Osmosis church is that such groups need to have a non-threatening title. Names like 'Agnostics Anonymous,' which can be very successful in Web churches, can be off-putting to many in the Osmosis church who consider themselves to be Christians already. Names such as 'Alpha Course' or 'Christian Basics' have been used with great success. I have come across churches, some describing themselves as liberal, where good numbers have come to faith through an annual 'School of Faith.' One evangelical Anglican church, with considerable numbers of new people moving in, holds a regular 'Welcome Course.' Many of those who do the course imagine themselves to be Christians when they start, but discover there is more to it as the course proceeds!

I do not have a completely clear answer to the question of whether 'hard' or 'soft' sell is the best solution for the general service fringe. I know of one

2 This is explored further in *Evangelism that Really Works*, chapter 3.

evangelical Anglican church where a new minister 'mopped up' the open fringe through gospel challenges at guest services. I have come across far more churches, though, where the 'soft sell' approach has worked best—low key invitations to a basics course, church membership class, or some such group. I have heard it suggested that new people should be invited to such groups within the first six months. After that, they can lose their openness. I cannot produce clear evidence to support this, but my instinct is that it is right.

Family Services

There is a myth that family (or all-age) services draw a fringe. My research indicates that the usual pattern of monthly family service, held at the standard service time and involving the normal weekly congregation, is largely *ineffective* in drawing a fringe. A *weekly* all-age service, though, and sometimes a monthly one held at a different time, can be very effective indeed.

In a study of 74 churches holding such services, 67 of the churches held an all-age service for the usual morning congregation at the normal service time, approximately monthly. The average additional adult fringe was just six people. Two churches held a monthly family service at a different time, therefore attracting a different congregation. The average additional number of adults was 31. Five churches held a weekly family service. It was harder, in this case, to define the size of the 'fringe,' but the average number of adults was 108, and many of them had been drawn in by the weekly family service.

One of the most surprising findings for me from my research project was the effectiveness of the weekly family service in drawing new people in, particularly in working class areas. I have some theories as to why this is. First, many unchurched people feel uneasy about the children going out to Sunday School, where they may not know others in the group, and with the parents already feeling uneasy in church. Second, the teaching in a family service is likely to be more 'seeker-sensitive' to non Christians. Finally, a weekly all-age service which is specifically targeted to families can generate a much better 'family feel' than one at which most of the congregation are not families at all. I have seen this apply, particularly, for families with very young children. If the congregation are mainly other young couples with bawling babes, a visitor to church will not be embarrassed if his or her own toddler creates a din. In a mixed congregation, though, however many assurances are given that the rest of the congregation do not mind, there is bound to be some embarrassment.

Case Study

St Cuthbert's, Fulwood, is a large parish of 13,500 in Preston, Lancs. 50% of it is Urban Priority Area, and this is more than reflected in the congregation. At the time of researching there were only 30 wage earners in the congregation, yet 350 adults attended church on a Sunday - reflecting 300% growth over seven years. Numbers at the weekly family service fluctuate, but have grown from an average of about 90 to nearly 300 over five years.

The family service lasts an hour, and has gone through different phases. Much of the time it was split into three sections. The first section was geared to the 5-8s, and included a story time when they came to the front. The next section covered the same theme, but was geared to the 9-14s, and always included a sketch or some other zany activity. The service finished with a seven minute talk to the adults which underlined some of the teaching earlier in the service.

At the time of writing there has been a change. Three Sundays in the month those nine and under leave the service after 15 minutes to have separate teaching of their own, though on the same theme as the rest of the service. One could argue that it is no longer an all-age service. The point is that it has acquired so strong a 'family flavour' that it still appeals to working class families, even though it has reverted to a standard Sunday School pattern.

An important aspect of the service has been its experiential flavour. For example, one service with a missionary theme involved the congregation circulating round five different groups in the church. One group was taking an engine apart, another was a Bible study, another had teaching about caring for babies, the fourth was a school class, and the final one was carpentry—making a cross. The service resulted in a dramatic increase in support for a missionary couple.

I asked Martyn Cripps, the vicar at the time, why the weekly family service had been so successful. There were two main reasons. It was culturally relevant—and the children gave the adults an 'excuse' for coming to church, particularly when the children were involved in some activity. Secondly, the children formed an effective network for drawing in friends. They brought their friends, and the friends, in turn, brought their parents.

Baptism Contacts

Many clergy find baptism follow-up a frustrating business. Whether their policy is tight or open, they find that the number of couples who start attending church regularly and find a real faith is depressingly low. Yet I have come across a number of churches which have found up to twenty per cent of baptism couples coming to faith. In some churches almost the whole congregation have come in through baptism enquiries! What is the secret?

I have found two main 'ways in.' The first is through a 'user-friendly' service.

Case Study

St Andrew's, Goldsworth Park, is a large estate of predominantly private housing on the edge of Woking, a London commuter town in Surrey. The church has a modern building, with its own coffee house, in the centre of the estate next to the Waitrose car park.

The 9.30 am Sunday Special service has around 45 adults and 30 or 40 children, mostly below the age of seven. Few had strong previous church links and nearly all of them have come as a result of baptism enquiries for the children. They mostly come as couples. The service lasts just over half an hour, and is led on a rota basis by different lay teams.

I attended a service. It was easy to see how the new couples felt at home, in a modern building, with not too large a group of other young couples like themselves. They actually ***believed*** *that they did not mind if their baby cried! The service consisted of a mixture of songs led by a small guitar group, prayers, a reading and a short talk, for which the children came to the front. Some weeks, I understand, there is drama. Even though the service is lay led, it does need support by the clergy, and it was some years before there were an adequate number of lay teams. Nevertheless, I did not feel there was anything which most congregations, provided they had couples with children of the right age, could not achieve.*

Once the children reach around seven years old, many of the couples move on to a later service, which has a Sunday School.

I was so impressed by this half-hour service that, at one point in my research, I thought a very short service might be a necessity. At other churches, though, baptism couples are drawn in good numbers at the morning family communion, lasting up to an hour and a quarter. My tentative conclusion is that the feel of the service is the key factor, and this depends particularly on having a large enough percentage of other young couples in the congregation. If this condition is not met, one needs to consider starting a separate 'seeker targeted' family service.

The second approach is through using *Good News Down the Street*[3] *after* the baptism. Some churches use this as baptism preparation, but there is a difficulty with this. Inevitably, many of the couples will not be ready to make a serious Christian commitment at the end of the course, and this can result in disappointment for the teams and resentment from the couples. Michael Wooderson, the author of *Good News Down the Street*, uses the course as post-baptism follow-up. He sends a letter to all couples about a month afterwards telling them about the course and explaining that it can lead to confirmation if they so wish. About a fifth take it up, and since these are the ones who are most open, it avoids the difficulties just mentioned. Many become Chris-

3 A 6 week Bible study course for enquirers in their own home described in M Wooderson, *Good News Down the Street* (Grove Pastoral Series No 9, Nottingham: Grove Books).

tians as a result.

A few churches carry out the first three sessions of the course as baptism preparation, leaving it optional whether to complete the course. There needs to be some experimentation to see what works best in an area. I realize, of course, that the very approach of leading a couple to Christian commitment *after* they have said the promises makes a nonsense of the liturgy. I justify it pragmatically, but I accept that it is far from satisfactory. Space precludes a full discussion here.

Parent and Toddler Groups

Parent and toddler groups are the most common type of church-run community group, and I include them here to illustrate the issue of evangelism in such groups. It is often claimed that such groups are a great source of young mums, in particular, joining the church, but my researches suggest that this is not the case. In a study of 29 parent and toddler groups, I found that the average number of new Christians per year was only 0.3.

Yet there are *some* groups which do yield significant numbers of new Christians. I found several where, each year, four or five women were becoming Christians. What is their secret? In part, no doubt, it must be the general life of the group, and the love and spirituality of the leadership. Yet I am convinced there is more to it than this. There are splendid groups with loving and spiritual leaders who are yielding very few new Christians. In my opinion much has to do with strategy—the way the group is set up and structured. The following four essentials are based on a study involving detailed interviews with leaders of 15 successful groups.

1. An Agreed Evangelistic Aim

There is nothing surprising about this. Evangelism is never easy, and in the chaotic atmosphere of a toddler group, unless the aim is agreed by all the leaders, it is fairly obvious that no evangelism will result. This applies particularly where there are frequent team changes, where an original vision, if not clearly defined, will easily fade as the original leaders leave the group.

2. A Trained and Committed Team

I used to think that, in church groups, the ordinary Christian members would naturally share their faith. My research persuaded me that, generally, this is not true. Most of the Christian mums who came were looking for a break! Most of the groups where effective evangelism was happening had a team which met together and prayed together. Training, particularly in personal evangelism, also proved valuable in many cases.

3. A Small Enough Group

Several of the leaders I spoke to confirmed that, above a certain size, evangelism becomes more difficult. The larger the group, the more likely people are to split into smaller groups or cliques. One leader put the limit at 15, another at 25. I am not saying there are no successful groups larger than this, but such groups require much greater skill in building relationships by the team.

4. Appropriate 'Link Strategies'

We have seen that evangelism is generally a gentle process. As people's hearts are warmed by the Christian love they experience in a group, there needs to be some natural way for them to move further and investigate Christian faith in a non-threatening environment. The next step will vary depending on the type of group. In the case of parent and toddler groups, my studies suggest that a low key enquirers' group, usually with other women from the group rather than from the whole church, is the best next step. Many churches hope to get the young mums into Sunday worship, probably via a pram service, and then lead them to faith. I can only say that, apart from baptism contacts, I have not come across any group where this is working with any consistency. Husband opposition, coupled with the sheer hassle of getting very young children out on a Sunday morning, do not make this a viable option for most mums, particularly where there is a culture gap with the church. A midweek group with other mums they already know is usually a more realistic option.

All these points are argued in more detail in chapter five of *Evangelism that Really Works*, in which I go on the suggest that similar factors also apply in many other kinds of church community groups. In a youth club, for example, evangelism will be difficult unless there is a trained committed team, group sizes are kept small, and there is an appropriate 'next step' which does not require too big a jump for the young people.

6

Evangelizing the Personal Fringe

Most would accept that, in response to the advance of secularisation in recent years, the church has become more inward looking. It has found itself bound up with itself and a small fringe which feels at home in church culture, and finds it hard to break out. Yet the Personal fringe reaches everywhere—or, at least, to many parts which 'other lagers cannot reach'! Many secular and irreligious people know somebody who is a Christian.

The Personal fringe is already vital for evangelism and, arguably, this importance may increase as the Institutional fringe continues to decline. This may, in part, account for the growing strength of some Web churches. Even in the Osmosis church, however, friendships are extremely important for evangelism. There may not be so many people brought to church specifically by a friend, but friendships will still be a supporting factor.

According to the Churches Together in England (CTE) Evangelism Research Project, friends or family were the most important factor for 48 per cent of people in becoming Christians.[4]

Let us consider some approaches to evangelizing the Personal fringe.

Guest Services

A number of experienced evangelists have said to me that guest services are no longer as effective as they were. I am referring here to specially advertised services, often with a visiting evangelist as preacher, where the aim of the service is to challenge people to commit their lives to Christ, or at least join an enquirers' group. The fact is, in most cultural settings, congregations find it desperately difficult to invite their friends to such 'churchy' events. Of 34 churches in my research which answered the question on guest services, 13 arranged such services from time to time. If baptismal services are excluded, the average number of guests was only twelve. Yet in some contexts, they work splendidly. Out of 189 people in the research who became Christians through a guest service, 147 were from one church, Gerrard Street Baptist Church in Aberdeen, a city centre Web church with many students.

As with any evangelism using the Personal fringe, it is in this kind of church, whose members have many contacts, where the possibilities are greatest. In a separate survey with returns from 24 experienced members of the (Anglican) Fellowship for Parish Evangelism, respondents were asked to rate different types of evangelism from 1 to 5, where 5 meant very effective

4 J Finney, *Finding Faith Today* (Bible Society, 1992) p 36.

and 1 meant useless, for different cultures. They agreed that the city centre church was the best place for guest services with a score of 3.9. The other three contexts were an outer suburb (3.6), a small village (3.1), and an inner city council estate (2.3). Personally, I was a little surprised that the gap between the inner city church and the suburb was not greater.

One trend, mentioned by many, was for traditional guest services to be replaced by a more low key 'process' approach, often known as a 'seeker service.' Many readers will be familiar with this approach which has gained a great deal of publicity as a result of the enormous church growth experienced by the Willow Creek Community church in Chicago.[5] A seeker service is really half-way between a service of worship and a gospel presentation. There is usually an emphasis on drama and music followed by a talk, with only a little congregational singing and almost no prayer. The movement has done a great deal of good in encouraging us in the British church to be more 'seeker-friendly,' but there is a great deal of debate at the moment about whether actual 'seeker-targeted' (that is, services *primarily* geared to non-Christians) work in British culture. It is too early to judge the issue. Certainly, not every church could lay on such services with great regularity, as the needs for dramatic and other artistic input are quite demanding, and not every church has a preacher sufficiently gifted in communicating with a largely unchurched audience.

Where does this leave us as far as traditional guest services are concerned? Have they had their day? The general informed view from those I spoke to in the research was that, while they are harder to use effectively than they once were, they still have a role. It is vital, though, that they are used as part of an overall evangelism strategy. Except in the classic Web churches, there must usually be an in-between stage. For churches with an Institutional fringe, this may be one of the 'open doors' in chapter four. For those with a Personal fringe there will need to be 'Stepping Stones'—social or evangelistic events outside church. Part of the reason for this is to gain the confidence of the congregation, and part is to raise the interest of those who are to be invited. Without such a strategy, guest services will have limited results.

Social and Evangelistic Events

If you speak of 'evangelism' to many people in our churches they will immediately think of evangelistic events, such as dinners, pub evenings and the like. Yet repeated research has shown that such events are not very successful in their own right in helping people become Christians—though they can be an important supporting factor. In the CTE research, only four per cent said they became Christians as a direct result of an evangelistic event,

5 See for example P Simmonds, *Reaching the Unchurched* (Grove Evangelism Series No 19, Nottingham: Grove Books).

but 13 per cent said it was a supporting factor. The implication of this is that the prime role of such events is not to 'bring people into the Kingdom,' but to help them move forward in their spiritual journey. So the speaker at such events may be less important, particularly for men, than some other factors—discovering Christians are normal, for example, and building relationships which will enable them to feel at home when they come to church.

In my research project, ministers found that social events with no speaker were as valuable for evangelism as those with a talk. The average number of non-Christians attending was higher at the social events (30 compared with 20), but the evangelistic impact was rated as almost identical.

What we are seeing, I believe, can be expressed easily in terms of the models of church described in chapter three. We have seen that the Web model will only work well for churches evangelizing reasonably receptive (i.e. sociable) groups in centres of population. Otherwise, for more 'ordinary' churches, the appropriate model for evangelizing the Personal fringe is the Stepping Stones model. One strong advocate of this approach is Malcolm Potter, Baptist missioner for Essex. He bases his approach on three principles, which I believe contain more than a grain of truth:

a) If someone will come to three quality social events in a row, they will start coming to church.
b) If they come to church for three months, they will be willing to join an enquirers' group.
c) Of those who join an enquirers' group, a very high percentage will become Christians and continue in the faith.

Enquirers' Groups

Most readers will need little convincing of the importance of basics or enquirers' groups. They are one reflection of the increased emphasis on process evangelism in Britain in recent years. One of their weaknesses until recently, however, has been a failure to tap adequately into the Personal fringe. For most enquirers or 'Just Looking' groups, the members are mainly invited by the clergy or the leaders of the course. Recently, though, there has been a significant innovation. The Holy Trinity Brompton (HTB) *Alpha* Course has drawn in large numbers by encouraging church members, particularly those on the last *Alpha* Course, to bring their friends. At HTB, 200 non-Christians regularly attend such courses in addition to new Christians and others wanting their faith strengthened.

After only a couple of years, hundreds of such courses are being run across the country, as many readers will know. The course covers standard Christian basics topics, with a strong emphasis on the Holy Spirit. But the format is somewhat different from a usual enquirers' group. Instead of group discussion in a home, it consists of a time of worship and a talk, followed by splitting down for discussion in small groups. Frequently there is also a meal.

It will not be possible, here, to discuss the *Alpha* Course in any detail, or to debate why it has been so successful at HTB. The reason it has created such massive interest, though, must be because it has raised the prospect of churches experiencing geometric growth. The course at HTB has grown from a small group meeting in a curate's flat to hundreds meeting in a hall. Could this happen in your church and mine?

It is, of course, too early to say, but a key indicator must be whether even now, when most *Alpha* Courses are small, churches are finding that the members of one course are recruiting sufficient members for the next. Some are, but by no means all. I led one course, when I was at St Mary of Bethany in Woking, where the reverse happened. The course was greatly appreciated by those who came, and some became Christians as a result, but no-one had any friends they could bring to the next course. What was the reason? Was it something to do with the particular individuals we had on the course? I do not think so. We were in a London commuter town where exhausted office workers tumble off the train at 7.30pm, still with children to put to bed and meals to eat. Many of them had few friends in the area, and they had little time to socialize and make new contacts. Any evangelism working off the Personal fringe will be extremely difficult in places such as this.

Where does this take us? First, we need to recognize that, as with all Web strategies, the *Alpha* Course will be most successful in 'receptive populations,' where people have plenty of friends. Second, I believe that we should at least consider targeting *Alpha* Courses towards receptive groups. At Greenham, where I am now, our first course has been for young adults, mainly singles, in their twenties. It is going well. I do not know yet whether each course will generate people for the next—but at least there is a chance.

The Christmas Fringe

The largest service fringe by far in virtually all churches is the Christmas fringe, yet very little is known about how to help these folk forward into faith. I have not researched it specifically, but I did not feel I could duck it in a book such as this on evangelizing the fringe. If only 10 per cent of those who come to church once a year, at Christmas, could be led into faith, it would revolutionize most of our churches. What can be done?

We are dealing, of course, with a mixture of Institutional and Personal fringe. I have left the Christmas fringe till last because it is the most open-ended of the examples. I shall simply offer a framework for considering the problem, and also share one or two nuggets I have picked up.

The framework is this. We need to distinguish between the Open fringe and the Closed fringe. In my experience, most of the extra people at midnight communion, for example, are closed. They have come as far as they wish to. I have heard of the occasional person being wonderfully converted though these services, but I have never heard of any church making a breakthrough—though I should be thrilled to hear if any reader knows otherwise.

Carol services such as 'Carols by Candlelight' are a little different. To be sure, many of the Institutional fringe who come are closed. These services, though, attract a higher number of friends of the congregation who are likely to be more open—the friendship link can be a key factor in evangelism. It follows, that to maximize the potential of adult carol services, one needs to major on the Personal fringe. When I was a curate at Holy Trinity, Leicester, a city centre Web church with a large Personal fringe, many of the congregation would bring their friends to the 'Carols by Candlelight' service. We always issued invitation cards, and one year the card invited people to the 'Carols by Candlelight' service 'followed by…' with space for church members to insert personal details such as 'mince pies and mulled wine at x's house.' Over about three years numbers increased from 300 to 700, and the church had to run two carol services to get everyone in. A number came to faith in this way.

One point which some experienced evangelists have made to me is that, in their opinion, many clergy are too hesitant in their evangelism at carol services. It *is* possible to preach for conversion, and I have known nurture groups started following such services—not as a result of my preaching, I must add! It needs a gifted speaker to get the right 'feel for the occasion' and at the same time preach a gospel message with a cutting edge. Some can do it. It is an opportunity not to be missed.

A third type of Christmas fringe is the family service fringe. Crib Services, Toy Services and Christingle Services, for example, attract many otherwise unchurched families. In my experience these are much more open than the midnight communion folk! A proportion are willing to start coming to a suitable family service throughout the year.

If I am right, the conclusion is obvious. We need to put our resources where the Open fringe are. We need to focus on the Personal adult fringe together with the family service fringe.

What other small nuggets do I have? I have heard of people being drawn in to enquirers' or 'Just Looking' groups simply by advertising them attractively at the Christmas services. I have also heard of evangelistic events being held in the Christmas season, and thereby drawing in extra people. The thought at first horrified me. I have enough to do in the lead up to Christmas without laying on extra evangelistic dinners and the like! The point is that such events can be organized early in December nowadays, and still be considered part of the Christmas season. Many groups in the church already organize their own Christmas events. Could some of these not be combined, or at least given a more outward-looking flavour?

7
Towards a Strategy

Evangelism is a social process—backed by prayer, certainly, and permeated by the Spirit of God—but it is still a social process. The church can organize itself in ways which assist this process or it can erect barriers.

The fringe forms the point of contact between the church and the community. As such, it is 'where the rubber hits the road' as far as evangelism is concerned. Relating rightly to the fringe is at the heart of evangelism strategy.

Needless to say, it is not the *only* issue which needs addressing. There are many ways in which a church can block growth—through dull services, poor organisation, bad leadership. These are beyond the scope of this book. A mission audit can, of course, be invaluable for providing a critical look at a church's mission on either a wide or a narrow front. In this booklet, though, we limit ourselves to the fringe. I should like to suggest four steps for producing a strategy.

1. Understand the Path to Faith

It will be necessary to understand why people have come into faith and joined the church in the recent past. What is the underlying evangelistic dynamic? Has the church been operating as a Web or Osmosis model—or is there some other underlying process which can be discerned. Critical to this will be the fringe. Have most of the new converts come from the Personal or the Institutional fringe? Why? If the church is only drawing in through the Personal fringe, is it turning off those in the local community in some way? Likewise, if the success is all coming through the Institutional fringe, why is it that church members are not bringing more of their friends? Is it a problem of spirituality or motivation? Or do we need to face the fact that, realistically, the present church members simply do not have friends to bring?

2. Analyse the Target Population

Having looked at what has happened in the past, we need to examine the population from which, in theory, the church should be drawing. How is the local population made up? What is the age and social mix? This can be found out through a local survey, or from the small area census statistics from the local library. The predominant group in my own parish, in Greenham, is families with children and teenagers. Yet these are poorly represented in the church. We need to understand how such a situation has come about.

Alternatively, does the church see itself as drawing from a wider population than its own parish? In that case, which groupings is it likely to attract, bearing in mind the ministry of other churches?

At this stage, much thought and prayer will be needed. Is there a mismatch between those who have recently joined the church, and the natural target population? If so, some hard choices may need to be made. Consider, for example, a church plant on a large council estate, with a predominance of young families. The first group to be attracted may well be elderly folk, with some church background in years past. One strategy would be to gear the church's ministry to this group. 'These are the people God is sending us.' Services would have a traditional flavour. This approach would probably yield the best results in the short term, but there would be a danger of creating a core group in the church which could never form a viable base for evangelizing the young families. An alternative strategy might be to provide something for the older ones—maybe a 'Songs of Praise' evening service, or even a midweek club and worship service, but to target the prime Sunday morning spot towards the young families, even if at first this service was poorly attended.

3. Assess the Church's Resources

Evaluate, realistically, the church's resources. Many target groups require some specialist skills. You do not have to be an expert to set up a family service but there does need to be someone in the congregation with at least some skills in that area. The same can be said of youth. Once again, thought and prayer will be needed. If there is a mismatch between resources and 'market needs,' will someone need to be recruited? At Greenham, I believe we have a good opportunity with youth. We have some exceptionally gifted and committed youth workers, but there are very few of them. They simply cannot do all the visiting and one-to-one work that they would like. As a result, we are considering arranging a team of volunteer young people to come to the church to strengthen our ministry in this area. Once a clear need is identified, it is remarkable, with prayer, how resources can be found.

4. Choose your Best Approach

Identify specific strategies. If the prime opportunity is seen to be the Institutional fringe, at least one 'open door' will need to be found. Some suggestions were made in chapter four. There will need to be commitment to it, and resources will need to be allocated.

Are there Web strategies which can be employed? These need not imply that the church as a whole is operating on such a model, but there may be local friendship networks which can be tapped into—children in a local school, youth, or a twenties 'scene'? If so, positive action will need to be taken. Special services, events, or possibly an Alpha Course will need to be arranged.

This process of finding suitable tactics to fulfil the overall strategy is by no means easy. Evangelism never is, except on paper! One difficulty is that the range of diversity in different churches and cultures is so great that it is far from easy to base what should happen on the experience of another church. One might retreat into super-spirituality and say 'we'll let the Lord lead us,' but unfortunately he does normally expect us to do our homework! In my opinion, we must be as thorough as possible in our research. Books can be valuable, and *Evangelism that Really Works* contains a much wider range of case examples than this one. Best of all, though, is to find another church which is as similar as possible to your own, but has moved further in its evangelism. Diocesan or other staff may be helpful. I can testify to the value of visiting churches where evangelism is really working, and where they don't mind answering awkward questions. My research project has strengthened my own faith, and given me renewed vision.

8
Conclusion

Many churches undervalue their fringe. In part, it is easy to see why. It is a natural group process for the most committed to look with some disdain at those who seem half-hearted. Nevertheless, we need to see it differently. The fringe—or some of them, at least—could be the committed Christians of tomorrow. What is more, they can be an invaluable 'way in' to the local community.

It is vital for a church to engage with its fringe in the most appropriate way. Failure to do so can cripple a church's evangelism. One important factor will be the pattern of relationships existing, or which could exist, between the church and its local community. This pattern will amount to an underlying evangelism dynamic, and we have expressed some of the most common patterns in terms of four models—the Osmosis, Web, Open Door and Stepping Stones.

There is no simple answer to finding the way forward, even when the evangelism dynamic has been identified. The experience of other churches can be a great help, combined with prayer. Some examples have been given in chapters four and five.